SOUND OF SILENCE

SOUND OF SILENCE

A Path to Inner Journey with Buddha Quotes

**COMPILED AND EDITED BY:
DR. SINGARA VADIVEL**

Sound of Silence....

Copyright© 2020 by **Singara Vadivel**

Book and Cover design: **Somesh Sharma S** and **Ashiq Wahab**

All rights reserved. This book may not be reproduced in whole or in part, or transmitted in any form, without written permission from publisher, except by reviewer who may quote brief passage in a review; nor may any part of this book reproduced, stored in retrieval system, or transmitted in any form or by any means electronic, mechanical, photocopying, recording, or other, without written permission from the publisher.

Sound of Silence: A Path to Inner journey with Buddha Quotes

Dr. Singara Vadivel, Ph.D.

First U.S printing, February 2020

ISBN: 9798608017735

Imprint: Independently published

Dedication:

To Everyone who gave me unbearable sufferings and to all my failures...

- Singara Vadivel

Contents

Preface vi

Acknowledgment: viii

Forward: Taking a Buddha lesson each day will serve you well -- David Nelson x

Forward: "Sound of Silence" deserves to be clubbed in the same league as Thirukkural – Dr. Nagarajan xii

Forward: "Sound of Silence" is a collection of life-changing thoughts and not a one time read as it guides throughout life -- Chandra Ragimanu & Sruthi xv

Chapter 1: Wisdom 2

Chapter 2: Love and Relationship 11

Chapter 3: About Life 27

Chapter 4: Motivation 37

Chapter 5: Inspirational 44

Chapter 6: About Success 49

Chapter 7: Peace and Worry 61

Chapter 8: Anger 69

Chapter 9: Karma 72

Chapter 10: Meditation 75

Chapter 11: Life Lesson 77

Chapter 12: Positive Mind 83

Chapter 13: Loneliness 87

Chapter 14: Happiness 89

Chapter 15: Mind and Mindfulness 98

Preface

"Suffering is not holding you; you are holding suffering."

"The things that hurt you the most, teach you the greatest lessons in life, Observe..."

"Ships don't sink because of the water around them. Ships sink because of the water that gets in them. Don't let what's happening around you get inside you and weigh you down."

"Relationship never dies a natural death. They always murdered by ego, attitude, and ignorance."

"You will not be punished for your ANGER; you will be punished by your ANGER."

--- Buddha

When life was really fluent and comfortable with worldly accomplishments, I never realized that it is completely enslaved with an egoic mind and holding out a phantom life with illusory identity. In the mind identified world, I have lost the ability to distinguish what is the actual value in life. The mind always sets an external entity as a destination in order to achieve felicity. Once the goal is reached, the happiness was short-lived and needed constant feeding in order to maintain the unquenchable mind thrust. Our mind is constantly looking for salvation. It becomes an unwinnable war with the mind to convince the true salvation is within, not without.

A few years ago, when my life's journey was faced with unexpected turbulence, everything had turned upside down and I had lost everything, including my worldly relationships, possessions, social status, identity, and confidence. Life completely knocked me down, so getting up and continuing my life's journey became unbearable, with pain with utter confusion. But sometimes we need bad things to happen to inspire, to change and grow. Maybe that's why they are happening. When life hit me hard, I was desperate to hold on and get up again, by overcoming human emotions. It took extreme mental and physical suffering to realize that Life begins at the end of the comfort zone.

During those extreme sufferings, these Buddha quotes were my driftwood to cross to the other side of the shore, and the reason why you are now holding this book. I am not the author of these quotes, I just compiled them from various sources. This represents a collection that was compiled over a long period of time. It was completed in book form in order to share with others the same strength and realization I had during my sufferings. I am not deserving nor do I expect any credit for any positive impact it may create, all the credit goes to either Buddha or whoever created these wonderful quotes in the name of Buddha. There is no evidence that all of these are the real teachings of Buddha. However, it makes them no less meaningful and important as real life-changing teachings. Instead of researching the origin, just taste it. I have reached a point where I have no need to impress anyone, for I have started the taste of real freedom.

What about you?

Dr. Singara Vadivel, Ph.D.
Austin – Texas
USA
singara.vadivel@gmail.com

Acknowledgment:

"A real friend is one who walks in when the rest of the world walks out"

---- Walter Winchell

"In everyone's life, at some time, our inner fire goes out. It is then burst into flame by an encounter with another human being. We should all be thankful for those people who rekindle the inner spirit."

--- Albert Schweitzer

I would like to convey my gratitude to my friends who stayed with me during a tough time in my life.

David Nelson (Gross & Nelson Attorneys at Law – Austin, Texas) - My best friend, Mentor, and Tennis coach, patiently listening to all my philosophical blabbering without disputing a single word. But of more importance to me was his constant support during my hard time.

Dr. Nagarajan and Dr. Kalamani (Principal, CIET, Coimbatore, Tamil Nadu, India)

Saravana Kumar and **Ananthi Selvi** (San Antonio, Texas)

Dr. Satish Thirumalai (La Frontera Dental – Austin, Texas)

Sethu Ramalingam (Chennai, Tamilnadu, India)

Srinika Saravanamuthu (Edmond, Oklahoma) - My favorite niece, who allowed me to revel my childish behavior from time to time.

Thank you Guys from my heart...

Forward: Taking a Buddha lesson each day will serve you well -- David Nelson

When my good friend Singara Vadivel asked me to write the forward to "Sound of Silence - A Path to inner Journey with Buddha Quotes", I was very honored. We have a lot in common. We are tennis partners, playing at least once a week, something we have done consistently for over 14 years. We both share the love of this great sport of tennis and it formed the initial bond between us that has endured all these years. But little did I know when we began our tennis experience how much it would evolve into a purposeful and deeply meaningful friendship, and how much I would learn from Singara about life's lessons derived from the teachings of Buddha.

Singara grew up in India, under extremely challenging economic conditions. His village was a very poor one, and he once commented that one sign of wealth was the transition from a thatched roof on his home to a more permanent tiled one. He owned no shoes until he went to college, but his upbringing has instilled in him the deepest sense of appreciation, a love of life without any need for material things. He exhibits a constant inner peace and he attributes much of it to his study of Buddha and the philosophy of Buddhism, so it is only appropriate he chose to write this book as a collection of Buddha sayings.

Growing up in a totally Christian environment, I was slow to adapt to his ideas and ideology, but frequently during our tennis breaks, when we paused to rest from the Texas summer heat, Singara would educate me in the ways of Buddha. I became a willing and avid listener, largely because I was clearly learning from someone who not only talked the talk but truly walked the walk. He exemplified everything Buddha represented in how one should live their lives, and it was only after reading this book that I fully appreciated how true that was..

This is not a traditional storybook, with plot and characters and a unique writing style that might be praised for its literary excellence, but rather what can serve as a daily reminder of what is truly important in life. Thus, it is a book that can be read over and over again. It never grows old and never becomes boring.

Starting my day flipping through a few pages and reflecting on one of the more appropriate sayings that grab my attention, I have come to appreciate just how wise the Buddha was and how much this troubled and often divided world could benefit from a regular dose of Buddha teachings. I highly recommend that you make it a regular part of any day, as impactful as that healthy diet, daily exercise regimen, restful sleep and all those other things we now are told will contribute to our extended health and happiness. I think you will find, as I have, that taking a Buddha lesson each day will serve you well.

David Nelson
Gross & Nelson Attorneys at Law
Austin - Texas,
USA

Forward: "Sound of Silence" deserves to be clubbed in the same league as Thirukkural – Dr. Nagarajan

"THIRUKKURAL" written by the great sage Thiruvalluvar, is a collection of meaningful couplets describing the modalities to be followed by any individual as well as the rulers. It covers all the aspects & concepts essential to lead a noble life and in making this world a better place.

Dr. Singara Vadivel's "SOUND OF SILENCE, A Path to Inner Journey with Buddha Quotes …" has been written on similar lines and it deserves to be clubbed in the same league as Thirukkural. It covers all the worldly affairs like., wisdom, love, relationship, motivation, inspirational anger, karma, meditation, etc.,

I am one of the persons who have been closely associated with him, understand the hardships and trauma he underwent a few years ago. He himself has mentioned it in his introduction. After thousands of soldiers were killed during the Mahabaratha war, the world got the priceless Bagavath Geetha. In a similar manner, Dr. Singara Vadivel, after the agony and suffering he experienced in his life, has given this world a beautiful book, which is the compilation of Buddha's quotes. Surely, if anyone follows at least some of these quotes in his/her life, it will be good for them.

The readers may be a bit skeptical of the application of these concepts in real life as no one can ever reach even one-millionth of

Buddha's quality. For those doubters, I have given the following anecdote.

When Abraham Lincoln gave his inaugural speech after becoming president of America, the egoistic people who could not accept a shoemaker's son as the president, posed the following question sarcastically: "Mr. Lincoln, you should not forget that your father used to make shoes for my family." And everyone in the Senate laughed. But Lincoln replied politely. "Sir, I know that my father used to make shoes for your family, and there will be many others here because he made the shoes the way nobody else can.

He was a creator. His shoes were not just shoes; he poured his whole soul into them. I want to ask you, have you any complaints? Because I know how to make shoes myself. If you have any complaints, I can make you another pair of shoes. But as far as I know, nobody has ever complained about my father's shoes. He was a genius; a great creator and I am proud of my father."

The whole Senate was struck dumb. They could not understand what kind of man Abraham Lincoln was. He was proud because his father did his job so well, with so much enthusiasm, passion, and perfection. The moral of this anecdote is that no one can hurt you without your consent. It is not what happens to us that hurts us; it is our response that hurts us.

"Ships don't sink because of the water around them; ships sink because of the water that gets in them. Don't let what's happening around you get inside you and weigh you down" (Page No.7 Chapter 1 Wisdom, Sound of Silence)

Last but not the least; I would suggest the author bring another book quoting an anecdote for each of Buddha's quotes. It will be quite interesting and make the readers realize his concepts better.

Dr. N. NAGARAJAN, Ph. D.
Principal
Coimbatore Institute of Engineering and Technology
Coimbatore,
Tamilnadu State
India

SOUND OF SILENCE

Forward: "Sound of Silence" is a collection of life-changing thoughts and not a one time read as it guides throughout life -- Chandra Ragimanu & Sruthi

Writing a Foreword for the book SOUND OF SILENCE is an Honour for us. We met Singara vadivel a year back and quickly became good friends. He perceives the simplicity of life by the principles of Buddhism and executes with great passion. The way he overcomes the hardship and the challenges of life is impressive and what he is today is very inspiring. He is generous and compassionate towards all living things. We share a common interest in life philosophy and had numerous discussions on Buddhist Principles.

"A positive thought ignited in a person's mind can lead to their destiny"

"Watch your thoughts, they become your words;
watch your words, they become your actions;
watch your actions, they become your habits;
watch your habits, they become your character;
watch your character, it becomes your destiny."

This book is a collection of Buddhist quotes that can build a reader's character. It is a collection of life-changing thoughts and not a one time read as it guides throughout life. The essence of the quotes is that they express a truth or an insight in a short and often amusing way. The beauty of this book is that it crosses all boundary lines of age, economics, race, religion, and education.

The quotes like "*Difficult roads often lead to beautiful destinations*" are thought-provoking and prepares one to take up
challenges. Thoughts expressed concisely have tremendous power, they can inspire, motivate and they can get a message across.

Mr. and Mrs. Chandra Ragimanu & Sruthi
Richmond, Virginia
USA

Chapter 1: Wisdom

- The root of suffering is attachment.

- Even death is not to be feared by one who has lived wisely.

- If anything is worth doing it with all your heart.

- A man is not called wise because he talks and talks again but if he is peaceful, loving, and fearless then he is in truth called wise.

- In a race between lion and deer often the deer wins. Because the line runs for food and the deer runs for life. The purpose is more important than need.

- All that we are is the result of what we have thought.

- Irrigators channel waters, fletchers straighten arrows, carpenters bend wood, the wise master themselves drop by drop is the water pot filled, likewise, the wise man, gathering it little by little fills himself with good.

- Better than a thousand hollow words, is one word that brings peace.

- If you knew what I know about the power of giving, you would not let a single meal pass without sharing it in some way.

SOUND OF SILENCE

- Silence the angry man with love, silence the ill-natured man with kindness, silence the miser with generosity, silence the liar with truth.

- People with opinions just go around bothering each other.

- Even as a solid rock is unshaken by the wind so are the wise unshaken by praise or blame

- You yourself must strive, Buddhas only point the way.

- Understanding is the heartwood of well-spoken words.

- Ceasing to do evil, cultivate the good, purifying the heart.

- Ardently do today, what must be done. Who knows? Tomorrow, death comes.

- Purity and impurity depend on oneself; no one can purify others.

- What you are is what you have been. What you'll is what you do now.

- If you find no one to support you on the spiritual path, walk alone.

- The quieter you become, the more you can hear.

- Tomorrow never comes, it is always today.

- Always HOPE but never expect.

- The stillness, the ruler of movement.

- There is no outside of you. It's all an inside game.

- Hate is heavy. Let it go.

- The greatest prayer is patience.

- 95% of your life is created by your subconscious mind.

- One of the best lessons you can learn in life is to master how to remain calm.

- You only live once... False! You live every day. You only die once.

- No matter how hard the past, you can always begin again.

- Never show your weakness to the world. Because the world is much interested to play with it.

- If you propose to speak, always ask yourself, is it true, is it necessary, it is kind.

- P.A.I.N.S – Positive Attitude in Negative Situations.

- Change is never painful, resistance to change is painful.

- Don't stress over what you can't control.

- We close our eyes when we pray, cry, dream because most beautiful things in life are not seen, but felt by the heart.

- By the accident of fortune, a man may rule the world for a time, but by virtue of love and kindness, he may rule the world forever.

- I can explain it to you, but I can't understand it for you.

- Arguing with a fool is like killing the mosquito on your cheek. You might kill it or not, but you'll end up slapping yourself for sure.

- Three things cannot be long hidden the sun the moon and the truth.

- How people treat you is their KARMA; How you react is yours.

- To cure of suffering, free yourself from attachment. Attachment is the source of all sufferings.

- Control your "ANGER" because it is just one letter away from "D" ANGER.

- Do not let the behavior of others destroy your inner peace.

- Nothing ever exists entirely alone; everything is in relation to everything else.

- Wounds are healed only when we touch them with compassion.

- I have no time to battle egos and small minds

- There is no fear for one whose mind is filled with desires.
- Be patient, everything will come to you at the right moment.
- Everything is temporary.
- Nothing ever goes away until it teaches us what we need to know.
- A person's energy can tell you more about them than their own words.
- Suffering is not holding you; you are holding suffering.
- Work out your own salvation. Do not depend on others.
- The things that hurt you the most, teach you the greatest lessons in life, Observe.
- Don't be slaves to your thoughts. Control them
- Always speak how you feel and never be sorry for being real.
- We walk this earth together, but the spiritual journey is walked alone.
- No matter how educated, talented, rich, or cool you believe you are, how you treat people ultimately tells all. Integrity is everything.

- Respect is earned. Honesty is appreciated. Trust is gained. Loyalty is returned.

- Use things, not people, Love people, not things.

- Truth is like a surgery. It hurts but cures. The lie is like a pain killer. It gives relief but has side effects forever.

- The best way to predict the future is to create it.

- Ships don't sink because of the water around them. Ships sink because of the water that gets in them. Don't let what's happening around you get inside you and weigh you down.

- Not everyone understands your journey. That's okay. You're here to live your life, not to make everyone understand.

- Use your voice for kindness, your ears for compassion, your hands for charity, your mind for truth, and your heart for life.

- When you are wrong, admit it. When you are right, be quiet.

- Don't mix bad words with your bad mood. You'll have many opportunities to change a mood, but you'll never get the opportunity to replace the words you spoke.

- When you die, they won't remember your car or house. They will remember who you were. Be a good human, not a good materialist.

- Live without pretending, Love without depending, Listen without defending, Speak without offending.

- Believe in yourself, and no one and nothing can stop you.

- Every morning we are born again. What we do today is what matters most.

- Some people suddenly change. One day you are important, the next day you're worthless.

- Before you assume, learn the facts. Before you judge, understand why. Before you hurt someone, feel. Before you speak, think.

- If you want to be powerful educate yourself.

- A random act of kindness, no matter how small, can make a tremendous impact on someone else's life.

- Just as a candle cannot burn without fire, men cannot live without a spiritual life.

- Expect nothing and appreciate everything.

- It is impossible that one engages in sensual pleasures without sensual desires, without perceptions of sensual desire, without thoughts of sensual desire.

- The Dhamma is similar to a daft, being for the purpose of crossing over, not for the purpose of grasping.

- Even if low-down bandits were to sever you limb from limb with a two-handled saw, anyone who had a malevolent thought on that account would not be following my instructions.

- Just as a mother would protect her son, her only son, with her own life, so one should develop toward all beings a state of mind without boundaries. And towards the whole world, one should develop loving-kindness, a state of mind without boundaries, about, below, and across, unconfined, without enmity, without adversaries.

- Be your own island, your own refuge, with no other refuge. Let the teaching be your island and your refuge, with no other refuge.

- You yourselves must strive; the Buddhas only point the way.

- Always be thankful for what you have, many people have nothing.

- We do not heal the past by dwelling there. We heal the past by living in the present.

- They say the people who exhibit the most kindness have experienced a lot of pain. The ones who act like they don't need love are the ones who need it more. The ones who take care of everyone else needs to care the most. And the people who smile may be the ones who cry when nobody is around.

- Some of the best advice you'll ever get will come from your gut instinct.

- Buddhism is a philosophy of life. Not a religion.

- When you have control over your thoughts, you have control over your life.

- Stop expecting. Start accepting life becomes much easier.

- This to pass. It may pass like a kidney stone, but it will pass.

- Believe what your heart tells you. Not what others say.

- No one notices your tears, no one notices your sadness, no one notices your pain, but they all notice your mistakes.

- One of the happiest moments of your life is when you find the courage to accept what you can't change.

- There are only two mistakes one can make along the road to truth not going all the way. And not starting.

Chapter 2: Love and Relationship

- Love doesn't need to be perfect. It just needs to be true.

- Love is not between a beautiful man and a woman. Love is between two beautiful hearts.

- Don't change so people will like you. Be yourself and the right people will love the real you.

- 3 words better than "I LOVE YOU" are "I TRUST YOU"

- Real love begins where nothing is expected in return.

- Remember, anyone can love you when the sun is shining. In the storms is where you learn who truly cares for you.

- When love is real, it finds away.

- Distance doesn't separate people, silence does.

- You don't need someone to complete you, you only need someone to accept you completely.

- Spend your time on those that love you unconditionally, don't waste it on those that only love you when conditions are right for them.

- It takes three seconds to say "I love you", three hours to explain why, and a lifetime to prove.

- Never argue with a liar. You can't win, because they believe their own lies.

- True love and a real friend are two of the hardest things to find.

- When wrong people leave your life, the right things start happening.

- The relationship never dies a natural death. They always murdered by ego, attitude, and ignorance.

- A good relationship is when someone accepts your past, supports your present, and encourages your future.

- He who loves 50 people has 50 woes, he who loves no one has no woes.

- Appreciate those who love you. Help those who need you. Forgive those who hurt you. Forget those who leave you.

- Do not get upset with people or situations, both are powerless without your reaction.

- One beautiful heart is better than a thousand beautiful faces.

- A real man does not love a million girls, he loves one girl in a million ways.

- Be with someone who is good for your mental health.

- Two things you'll never have to chase: True friends and true love.

- Don't believe those who tell you they love you, believe those who show you they do.

- True love is born from understanding.

- Break-up in love is Wake-up in Life.

- Love makes everything that is heavy, light.

- Make sure you love yourself before you start to love someone else.

- When the nail grows long, we cut nails not finger. Similarly, when misunderstanding grows up, cut your ego, not your relationship.

- Life doesn't always introduce you to the people you want to meet. Sometimes, life puts you in touch with the people you need to meet to help you, to hurt you, to leave you, to love you, and to gradually strengthen you into the person you were meant to become.

- A true relationship is when you can tell each other anything and everything. No secrets, no lies.

- No relationship is all sunshine, but two people can share one umbrella and survive the storm together.

- Never forget 3 peoples in life: 1) Who helped you in difficult times. 2) Who left you in difficult times. 3) who put you in difficult times.

- The problem with nice people is that they will not tell you that they are hurt, they will wait for you to realize your mistake.

- Why do we close our eyes when we pray, cry or dream? Because the most beautiful things in life are not seen but felt by the heart.

- Stop expecting loyalty from people who can't even give you honesty.

- Anyone can say they care. But watch their actions, not their words.

- Cut off fake people for real reason, not the real people for fake reasons.

- Never misuse the one who loves you, never say busy the one needs you, never cheat the one who really trusts you, never forget the one who always remembers you.

- Love is a gift of one's innermost soul to another so both can be whole.

- You, yourself, as much as anybody in the entire universe, deserve your love and affection.

- True love is like a falling start we don't know how and when and where it happens.

- Difference between like and love: when you like a flower, you just pluck it. But when you love a flower, you water it daily.

- Love relationships are not exams to pass or fail and not a competition to win or lose, but it's a feeling in which you care for someone more than yourself.

- People are not as beautiful as they look, as they walk, or as they talk. They are only as beautiful as they love, as they care and as they share.

- Without communication, there is no relationship, there is no love. Without trust, there's no reason to continue.

- A single moment of misunderstanding in love is so poisonous, that it makes us forget the hundred lovable moments spent together within a minute.

- You come to love not by finding the perfect person, but by seeing an imperfect person perfectly.

- No one in this world is pure and perfect. If you avoid people for their mistakes, you will be alone in this world. So, judge less and love more.

- Always remember, pain makes people change. So don't hurt them when you don't want them to change.

- You may fall in love with the beauty of someone, but remember that finally, you have to live with the character, not the beauty.

- True Love is not found. It is built.

- He who does not understand your silence will probably not understand your words.

- Don't trust people who tell you other people's secrets.

- Love is when the other person's happiness is more important than your own.

- Fall in Love with Souls, not faces.

- Immature people always want to win an argument, even at the cost of the relationship. Mature people understand that it's always better to lose an argument and win a relationship.

- Love when you are ready, not when you're lonely.

- Fall in love with a person who enjoys your madness. Not an idiot who forces you to be normal.

- Love is when you sit beside someone, doing nothing, yet you feel perfectly happy.

- Don't be a beggar of love, be the donor of life.

- beautiful people are not always good, but good people are always beautiful.

- Ego is just a small three-letter word, which can destroy a big twelve letter word called Relationship.

- A clear rejection is always better than a fake promise.

- One beautiful heart is more important than a million beautiful faces.

- If you really want to change the world, go home and love your family.

- When you give and expect a return that's an investment, but when you give and expect nothing that's pure love.

- True love has no expiration date.

- Love is not what you say. Love is what you do.

- Self-love is the greatest medicine.

- If you don't love yourself, you'll always be chasing after people who don't love you either.

- The best love is the one that makes you a better person, without changing you into someone other than yourself.

- Love is nothing without action. Trust is nothing without proof. And sorry is nothing without change.

- Real love is not based on romance, candlelight dinner, and walks along the beach. Real love is based on respect, compromise, care, and trust.

- When ego comes, everything else goes. When the ego goes everything else comes.

- Find someone who loves your soul more than your body.

- Love yourself first, because that's who you'll be spending the rest of your life with.

- Love is not blind. It's the attachment that makes us blind.

- A person that truly loves you will never let you go, no matter how hard the situation is.

- Don't ask why people keep hurting you. Ask yourself why are you allowing.

- Always listen to your heart, because even though it's on your left side, it's always right.

- Everything is temporary, so try not to get too attached.

- While you were waking up today, someone else was taking their last breath. Be thankful for this day. Don't waste it.

- Learn to love without condition. Talk without bad intention. Give without any reason. And most of all, care for people without any expectations.

- Don't react to toxic people. Not giving them a reaction when they desperately seek it, is far powerful.

- Strength grows when we dare. Unity grows when we pair. Love grows when we share. A relationship grows when we care.

- A good woman wants your Love, time and attention and not your money.

- Strong people don't put others down... they lift them up.

- Keep your circle small and your mind at peace.

- The most dangerous creature on the earth is a fake friend.

- Great minds discuss ideas; average minds discuss events; small mind discusses people.

- Sometimes you need bad things to happen to inspire you to change and grow. Maybe that's why they are happening to you.

- No one born with self-confidence. Self-confidence is learned and earned with experience.

- The secret to living well and longer is: eat half, walk double, laugh triple, and love without measure.

- Don't quit. Sometimes the things you are hoping for, come at unexpected times.

- There are 4 very important words in life: Love, Honesty, Truth, and Respect. Without these in your life, you have nothing.

- I am mature enough to forgive you, but not dumb enough to trust you again.

- Don't waste words on people who deserve your silence. Sometimes the most powerful thing you can say is nothing at all.

- The person you look for granted today may turn out to be the person you need tomorrow. Never look down on someone.

- Time decides who you meet in life, your heart decides who you want in your life, and your behavior decides who stays in your life.

- A relationship with a nice person is like sugarcane. You break it, crush it, squeeze it, even beat or grind it, still will get only sweetness.

- Just because I don't react, does not mean I did not notice.

- Life becomes easier when you delete the negative people from your life.

- Don't worry about what others think... Most people don't use their brain very often.

- Travel and tell no one, live a true love story and tell no one, live happily and tell no one. People ruin beautiful things.

- We never lose friends; we just learn who our real ones are.

- Once you feel you are avoided by someone, never disturb them again.

- How good or bad other people are, is their own business. Focus on your own business instead.

- Look within... the secret is inside you.

- The most important thing is to enjoy your life.

- Honesty is always one of the best keys to make a good relationship.

- What is coming is better than what is gone.

- Don't worry if people don't like you. Most people are struggling to like themselves.

- Be grateful for what you have, others might not be so blessed.

- Be the reason someone believes in the goodness of people.

- When you come to a point where you have no need to impress anybody, your freedom will begin.

- The ego wants quantity and the soul wants quality.

- Never ignore a person who loves you, cares for you and misses you. Because one day, you may wake up from your sleep and realize that you lost the moon while counting the stars.

- Everybody has their own struggles. So be kind.

- Your happiness and suffering depend on your actions not on my wishes for you.

- If you don't like something, change it. If you can't change it, change your attitude.

- You can't control how other people see you or think of you... and you have to be comfortable with that.

- A friend who understands your tears is much more valuable than a lot of friends who only know your smile.

- Forget your past, forgive yourself and begin again. It's never too late.

- Mistakes increase your experience and experience decrease your mistakes. If you learn from your mistakes then others learn from your success.

- Some people come to your life as blessings. Others come in your life as lessons.

- Do not let the behavior of others destroy your peace of mind.

- Mastering others is strength. But mastering yourself is true power.

- Complaining is finding faults. Wisdom is finding solutions.

- Never lie to someone who trusts you, and never trust someone who lies to you.

- A Fake friend is more dangerous than an enemy.

- Never leave a true relationship for a few faults. Nobody is perfect, nobody is correct. In the end, affections are always greater than perfection.

- Never cry for that person that hurt. Just smile and say thank you for giving me the chance to find someone better.

- Control your emotions or they will control you.

- I don't judge others, because I am not perfect.

- Easy is to judge the mistakes of others. Difficult is to recognize your own mistakes.

- My love is unconditional, but my trust and respect are not.

- I am not perfect, but at least I am not fake.

- Love is nothing without action. Trust is nothing without proof. And sorry is nothing without change.

- Love is not about possession. Love is about appreciation.

- Once in a lifetime, you meet someone who changes everything.

- If you get tired learn to rest, not to quit.

- Be a good person, but don't waste time to prove it.

- Apologizing does not always mean you're wrong and the other person is right. It just means you value your relationship more than your ego.

- Cheating on a good person is like throwing away a diamond and picking up a rock.

- Sometimes It's better to remain silent and smile.

- Missing someone is your heart's way of reminding you that you love them.

- Silence is better than unnecessary drama.

- Forgive them, even when they are not sorry.

- I have no time for gossip, distractions or negativity.

- Be happy you never know how much time you have left.

- If you don't like it when you walk, move you are not a tree.

- Let people judge you. Let them misunderstand you. Let gossip about you. What they think of you isn't your problem. Their opinions do not pay your bills. So you stay kind, committed to love, and free in your authenticity, and no matter what they do or say never doubt your worth or the beauty of your truth. You keep on shining and let the haters hate.

- Growth is painful. Change is painful. But nothing is as painful as staying stuck somewhere you don't belong.

- Difficult roads often lead to beautiful destinations.

- The family is in just blood and bones. It's the people who stood by you in the darkest times.

- "Karma," think good thoughts, say nice things, too good for others. Everything will come back.

- Honesty is a very expensive gift. Don't expect it from cheap people.

- Love is when the other person's happiness is more important than your own.

- How people treat other people is a direct reflection of how they feel about themselves.

- Keep your circle small and your mind at peace.

- A lot of problems in the world would disappear if we talk to each other instead of talking about each other.

- When you look for the good in others, you discover the best in yourself.

- Beauty is not in the face; beauty is a light in the heart.

- When another person makes you suffer, it is because he suffers deeply within himself, and his suffering is spilling over. He does not need punishment; he needs help. That's the message he is sending.

- Don't worry about what people say behind your back. They're the ones who find faults in your life instead of fixing their own.

- If they respect you, respect them. If they disrespect you, respect them. You represent yourself. Not others.

Chapter 3: About Life

- Life begins at the end of your comfort zone.
- Life is a beautiful lie and death is a painful truth.
- Definition of stupid: Knowing the truth, seeing the truth, but still believing the lies.
- I don't want a perfect life. I want a happy life.
- Judge me when you are perfect.
- Life always offers you a second chance. It's called Tomorrow.
- Trust is like a glass, once broken it will never be the same again.
- Never stop learning, because life never stops teaching.
- Stay patient and trust your journey.
- Life… It's a beautiful miracle.
- Wanting to be someone else is a waste of who you are.
- Turn your wounds into wisdom
- Severn Dangers to Human Virtue: 1) Wealth without work 2) Pleasure without conscience 3) Knowledge without

character 4) Commerce without morality 5) Science without humanity 6) worship without sacrifice 7) Politics without principle.

- A quiet mind and a kind heart are all you need.

- If I am wrong, educate me. Don't belittle me.

- The future depends on what we do in the present.

- What hurts you today, makes you stronger tomorrow.

- Forget what hurts you, but don't forget what it taught you.

- Don't take revenge. Let Karma do all the work.

- Life is really simple, but we insist on making it complicated.

- Right is right even if everyone is against it, and Wrong is wrong even if everyone is for it.

- Never say sorry for being honest.

- Purity or impurity depends on oneself; no one can purify another.

- Your beliefs don't make you a better person, but your behavior does.

- Do not educate your children to be rich. Educate them to be happy. So, when they grow up they will know the value of the things, not the price.

- All that we are is the result of what we have thought. The mind is everything. what we think we become.

- Thousands of candles can be lit from a single candle, and the lite of the candle will not be shortened. Happiness never decreases by being shared.

- You yourself, as much as anybody in the universe deserve your love and affection.

- Three things cannot be long hidden: The Sun, The moon, The truth.

- We are shaped by our thoughts, we become what we think. When the mind is pure joy follows like a shadow that never leaves.

- The only real failure in life is not to be true to the best one knows.

- You cannot travel the path until you have become the path itself.

- An idea that is developed and put into action is more important than an idea that exists only as an idea.

- When you realize how perfect everything is you will tilt your head back and laugh at the sky.

- However, many holy words you read, however many you speak, what good will they do you if you do not act on upon them.

- A jug fills drop by drop.

- The tongue like a sharp knife kills without drawing blood.

- Even death is not to be feared by one who has lived wisely.

- A dog is not considered a good dog because has a good barker. A man is not considered a good man because he is a good talker.

- There is nothing more dreadful than the habit of doubt.

- The way is not in the sky, the way is in the heart.

- Life and time are the world's best teachers. Life teaches us the use of time and time teaches us the value of life.

- Have compassion for all beings rich and poor alike each has their suffering, some suffer too much other too little.

- Teach this triple truth to all: A generous heart, kind speech and a life of service and compassion are the things which renew humanity.

- The whole secret of existence is to have no fear. Never fear what will become of you depend on no one, only the moment you reject all help are you freed.

- No one saves us but ourselves. No one can and one may. We ourselves must walk the path.

- The secret of health for both mind and body is not to mourn for the past worry about the future or anticipate troubles.

- Work out your own salvation. Do not depend on others.

- To conquer oneself is a greater than conquering others.

- To keep the body in good health a duty, otherwise, we shall not be able to keep our mind strong and clear.

- There has to be evil so that good can prove its purity about it.

- In Buddhism, there is no place for saving anybody.

- Buddha says, "I can show the way, but you have to walk. I can't walk for you. And if you don't want to walk who am I to force you to walk."

- Buddhism teaches that nothing happens by chance. Everything has meaning. Please be convinced that your inner life is already endowed with everything you need. No matter how difficult your situation may be, you are alive now, and there is no treasure more precious than life itself.

- Every human being is the author of his own health and disease.

- Hatred does not cease through hatred at any time. Hatred ceases through love. This is an unalterable law.

- Whatever words we utter should be chosen with care for people will hear them and be influenced by them for good or ill.

- All wrong-doing arises because of mind, if the mind is transformed can wrong-doing remain?

- In the sky there is no distinction between east and west, people create distinctions out of their own minds and then believe them to be true.

- Life is an echo. What you send out, comes back. What you sow, you reap. What you give, you get. What you see in others exists in you. Remember life is an echo. It always gets back to you.

- If we could see the miracle of a single flower clearly, our whole life would change.

- The greatest enemy in life... IS THE SELF.

- The greatest failure in life... IS NARCISSISM.

- The greatest tragedy in life... IS JEALOUSY

- The greatest fault in life... IS TO LOSE ONESELF.

- The greatest crime in life... IS DISLOYALTY TO PARENTS.

- The greatest ignorance in life... IS DECEIT.
- The greatest pity in life... IS SELF DEPRECIATION.
- The greatest pride in life... REVIVING FROM FAILURE.
- The greatest bankruptcy in life... IS HOPELESSNESS.
- The greatest wealth in life... IS HEALTH AND WISDOM.
- The greatest debts in life... IS OWING LOVE.
- The greatest gift in life... IS ACCEPTANCE AND FORGIVENESS.
- The greatest shortcoming in life... IS LACK OF AWARENESS.
- The greatest console in life... IS ENDOWMENT AND CHARITY.
- Some people want material things. Me, I just want Peace, happy times and people who love me.
- Only a positive attitude will give you a positive and successful life.
- Only you can change your life. No one can do it for you.
- Be patient. Everything comes to you at the right moment.
- My Religion is very simple. My religion is kindness.
- Second chances are rare, use your first wisely.

- Walking alone is not difficult. But when we walked a mile with someone, then coming back alone, that is more difficult.

- People will hurt you and then they act as you hurt them.

- Sun is alone, too, but it still shines.

- Don't worry about dying. Worry about not living.

- Don't blame people for disappointing you. Blame yourself for expecting too much from them.

- Do the right thing, even when no one is looking. It's called integrity.

- I stopped explaining myself when I realized people only understand from their level of perception.

- Six rules of Life: 1) Before you pray... Believe. 2) Before you speak... Listen. 3) Before you spend... Earn. 4) Before you write... Think. 5) Before you quit... Try. 6) Before you die... Live.

- You can't change how people feel about you, so don't try. Just live your life and be happy.

- Mistakes are proof that you are trying.

- A negative mind will never give you a positive life.

- Stay stronger, make them wonder how you are still smiling.

- The ego never accepts the truth.

- Never give up. Great things take time.

- Apologize for being wrong, not for being honest.

- Weak people revenge. Strong people forgive. Intelligent people ignore it.

- Not everyone will understand your journey. Just be yourself and carry on.

- I don't trust words. I trust actions.

- Don't believe in Luck. Believe in hard work.

- Don't worry about being perfect, just be honest

- The tongue has no bones but is strong enough to break a heart. So be careful with your words.

- Wrong is wrong even if everyone is doing it. Right is right even if no one is doing it.

- Open your mouth only if you are going to say is more beautiful than silence.

- When you focus on problems, you get more problems. When you focus on possibilities, you have more opportunities.

- Every man today is the result of his thoughts yesterday.

- If you can change your mind, you can change your life.

- Life is short, spend it with people who make you laugh and feel loved.

- Your best teacher is your last mistake.

- One of the best feelings in the world is knowing that someone is happy because of you.

- Silence is the best reply to a fool.

- All situations teach you, and often it's the tough ones that teach you the best.

- If you never tasted a bad apple, you wouldn't appreciate a good apple. You have to experience life to understand life.

- Learn to work alone. It will make you stronger.

- When you really pay attention, everything is your teacher.

Chapter 4: Motivation

- Everything is temporary.

- If you want to know your future, look at what you're doing at this moment.

- Only you can change your life. No one can do it for you.

- Never stop believing in hope because miraculous happened every day.

- Never make permanent decisions on temporary feelings.

- The best things in life come with patience and hard work.

- Silence and smile are two powerful words. A simile is the way to solve many problems and silence is the way to avoid many problems.

- Fall seven times, stand up eight.

- All birds find shelter during the rain. But the eagle avoids rain by flying above the clouds. Problems are common, but attitude makes the difference.

- If you have nothing in life but a good friend, you are rich.

- Open your mind before you open your mouth.

- I belong to no religion. My religion is LOVE. Every heart is my temple.

- Understanding is deeper than knowledge. There are many people who know you, but few who understand you.

- Continue to Love, continue to forgive, continue to grow.

- Do good and good will come to you.

- Being polite is so rare these days, that it's often confused with flirting.

- Four beautiful thoughts of life: Look back and get experienced, Look Forward and See Hope; Look around and find reality, and Look within and find yourself.

- One loyal friend is worth a thousand relatives.

- Hurting someone with truth is better than making them happy with a lie.

- When trust is broken, sorry means nothing.

- Never explain yourself to anyone. You don't need anyone's approval. Live your life and do what makes you happy.

- Do not dwell in the past, do not dream of the future, concentrate the mind on the present moment.

- To live a pure unselfish life, one must count nothing as one's own in the midst of abundance.

- Better than a thousand hollow words, is one word that brings peace.

- To forgive others is to be good to yourself.

- It is better to conquer yourself than to win a thousand battles.

- Attachment leads to suffering.

- The mind is everything. What you think you become.

- Happiness comes when your work and words are of benefit to yourself and others.

- Be strong but not rude. Be kind but not weak. Be bold but not bully. Be humble but not timid, be proud but not arrogant.

- If your religion requires you to hate someone you need a new religion.

- No storm can last forever. it will never last 365 days consecutively. Don't worry no storm, not even the one in your life, can last forever.

- Anything that costs you your peace is too expensive learn to let it go.

- If it comes; let it. If it goes; let it. Don't be attached and you will find peace.

- If you light a lamp for someone else, it will also brighten your path.

- Don't stop when you are tired, stopped when you're done.

- It's your mind that creates this world.

- Be kind to everything that lives.

- If you can't handle the stress you can't handle success.

- Let your past makes you better, not bitter.

- They will ignore you until they need you.

- The best revenge is not to be like your enemy.

- Overthinking ruins friendships and relationships. Overthinking creates problems you'll never have. Don't overthink, just to overflow with good vibes.

- Keep calm, because nothing lasts forever.

- The best revenge is no revenge. Just forget they exist.

- I woke up. I have clothes to wear. I have running water. I have food to eat. Life is good. I'm thankful.

- If we can find money to kill people, we can find the money to help.

- Wake up every morning believing today is going to be better than yesterday.

- Silence is sometimes the best answer.

- Time is like a river. You cannot touch the same water twice, because the flow that has passed will never pass again. Enjoy every moment of your life.

- Everything heals. Your body heals. Your heart heals. The mind heals. Wounds heal. Your soul repairs itself. Your happiness is always going to come back.

- Be kind to all creatures. This is the true religion.

- Not everyone will understand your journey. That's fine. It's not their journey to make sense of. It's yours.

- Do not be afraid to fail. Be afraid not to try.

- Who gossips to you, will gossip about you?

- Life has taught me that you can't control someone's loyalty.

- The six best doctors: sunshine, water, rest, air, exercise, and diet.

- Don't let yourself be controlled by 3 things: Money, people, or past experiences.

- Loyalty is hard to find. Trust is easy to lose. Actions speak louder than words.

- Love all. Trust few. Everything's real but not everyone's true.

- Always hope but never expect.

- Sometimes it's better to just remain silent, and smile.

- People come and go. The best ones stay.

- A strong person is the one who cries, then gets up and fights again.

- When something is gone. Something better is coming.

- people who don't understand your silence will never understand your words.

- Accept that you are not important to some people, and move on.

- Our prime purpose in this life is to help others. And if you can't help them, at least don't hurt them.

- I am 97% sure you don't like me, but I am 100% sure I don't care.

- Your life does not get better by chance, it gets better by change.

- Smile, it will make you feel better. Pray, it will keep you strong. Love, it will make you enjoy life.

Chapter 5: Inspirational

- If anything is worth doing, do it with all your heart.
- Everything that has a beginning has an ending. Make your peace with that and all will be well.
- All that we are is the result of what we have thought.
- What you think you become. What you feel you attract. What you imagine, you create.
- Nothing can harm you as much as your own thoughts unguarded.
- It is better to be hated for what you are than to be loved for what you are not.
- In the end, only three things matter: how much you loved, how gently you lived, and how gracefully you let go of things not meant for you.
- The greatest achievement is selflessness.
- The greatest worth is self-mastery.
- The greatest quality is seeking to serve others.
- The greatest precept is continual awareness
- The greatest medicine is the emptiness of everything.

- The greatest magic is transforming passion.
- The greatest generosity is non-attachment
- The greatest goodness is a peaceful mind.
- The greatest patience is humility.
- The greatest effort is not concerned with results.
- The greatest meditation is a mind that let go.
- No one saves us but ourselves. No one can and no one may. We ourselves must walk the path.
- Happiness or sorrow – whatever befalls you, walk on untouched, unattached.
- Each morning, we are born again. What we do today is what matters most.
- Don't rush anything, when the time is right, it'll happen...
- Your work is to discover your world and them with all your heart give yourself to it.
- The whole secret of existence is to have no fear.
- Health is the greatest gift, contentment is the greatest wealth, A trusted friend is the best relative, the liberated mind is the greatest bliss.
- You only lose what you cling to.

- The thought manifests as the word; the word manifests as the deed; the deed develops into habit, and habit hardens into character. So, watch the thought and its ways with care, and let it spring from love born out of concern for all beings.

- When we meet real tragedy in life, we can react in two ways: either by losing hope and falling into self-destructive habits or by using the challenge to find our inner strength.

- On the long journey of human life, Faith is the best companions.

- All human unhappiness comes from not facing reality squarely, exactly as it is.

- Those who are free of resentful thoughts surely find peace.

- When the student is ready the teacher will appear.

- It is during our darkest moments that we must focus to see that light.

- Quiet the mind, and the soul will speak.

- To understand everything is to forgive everything.

- Be kind to all creatures, this is the true religion.

- If your compassion does not include yourself, it is incomplete.

- Believe nothing, no matter where you read it or who has said it, not even if I have said unless it agreed with your own reason and your own common sense.

- If you want to fly, give up everything that weighs you down.

- Standing alone is better than being around people who don't value you.

- To be old and wise, you must first be young and stupid.

- Every end is a new beginning.

- Never give up. Today is hard, tomorrow will be worse, but the day after tomorrow will be sunshine.

- Kindness is the language which the deaf can hear and the blind can see.

- If you can stay positive in a negative situation, you win.

- Fear does not stop death, it stops life.

- When one door closes, another opens.

- Life is very short, so break your silly egos, forgive quickly, believe slowly, love truly, laugh loudly and never avoid anything that makes you smile.

- Believe in yourself, when everyone else doesn't.

- The strongest hearts have the most scars.

- Just as a snake sheds its skin, we must shed our past over and over again.

- You cannot heal in the same environment where you got sick.

- Never argue with a fool. People watching may not be able to tell the difference.

- Don't treat people as bad as they are, treat them as good as you are.

- Don't waste your time with explanations: people only hear what they want to hear.

- Don't talk Act. don't say, Show, don't promise Prove.

- No one is more hated than he who speaks the truth.

- The happiness of your life depends on the quality of your thoughts.

Chapter 6: About Success

- What is success? Success is being able to go to bed each night with your mind at peace.

- To succeed in life, you need three things: a wishbone, a backbone, and a funny bone.

- Without struggle, success has no value.

- If you want to be successful, you must respect one rule: Never lie to yourself.

- Every day is not a success. Every year is not a success. You have to celebrate the good.

- Success hugs you in private. Failure slaps you in public. That's life.

- The biggest adventure you can take is to live the life of your dreams.

- The best time for new beginnings is now.

- Failure is not the opposite of success; it's part of success.

- Those who don't believe in magic will never find it.

- The secret of success is to do the common thing uncommonly well.

- No one is you and that is your superpower.

- What comes easy won't last long, and what lasts long won't come easy.

- Whatever life plants you, bloom with grace.

- Lead from the heart, not the head.

- If you don't like the road you're walking, start paving another one.

- The secret to success is to know something nobody else knows.

- Believing yourself is the first secret to success.

- In order to succeed, we must first believe that we can.

- Love yourself first and everything else falls into line.

- Many of life's failures are people who did not realize how close they were to success when they give up.

- Successful people always have two things on their lips, 1) Silence 2) Smile.

- In order to succeed, your desire for success should be greater than your fear of failure.

- A successful man is one who can lay a firm foundation with the bricks that others throw at him.

- The difference between who you are and who you want to be is what you do.

- If you can dream it, you can do it.

- Every experience, no matter how bad it seems, holds within it a blessing of some kind. The goal is to find it.

- Never stop doing your best just because someone doesn't give you credit.

- Some people dream of success while others wake up and work.

- Success isn't just about what you accomplish in your life; it's about what you inspire others to do.

- Success is not the key to happiness. Happiness is the key to success. If you love what you are doing, you will be successful.

- If you really want to do something, you'll find away. If you don't, you'll find an excuse.

- Success seems to be connected with action. Successful people keep moving. They make mistakes, but they don't quit.

- All progress takes place outside the comfort zone.

- There are no secrets to success. It is the result of preparation, hard work, and learning from failure.

- The ones who are crazy enough to think they can change the world, are the ones that do.

- If you are not willing to risk the usual, you will have to settle for the ordinary.

- Success is walking from failure to failure with no loss of enthusiasm.

- Stop chasing the money and start chasing the passion.

- Never give in except to convictions of honor and good sense.

- Try not to become a man of success. Rather become of a man of value.

- Successful people do what unsuccessful people are not willing to do. Don't wish it were easier; wish you were better.

- Success usually comes to those who are too busy to be looking for it.

- Don't be afraid to give up the good to go for the great.

- Opportunities don't happen. You create them.

- The road to success and the road to failure are almost exactly the same.

- It is better to fail in originality than to succeed in imitation.

- It's not whether you get knocked down. It's whether you get up.

- When watching after yourself, you want after others.

- Everything you've ever wanted is on the other side of fear.

- Radiate boundless love towards the entire world above, below, and across.

- It does not matter how slowly you go as long as you do not stop.

- There is nothing comparable to one who is awakened.

- Success is not final; failure is not fatal: it is the courage to continue that counts.

- When things feel a bit dark and you're stuck in a bad patch.

- When you want to experience more good things in your life but you've been focused on the problems...

- When your soul has been feeling a little unhappy and you want an energy boost...

- Sometimes we're tested not to show our weakness, but to discover our strengths.

- When you want to take control of your life and make the most of everything around you...

- When good things are taking too long to manifest and you're starting to lose faith.

- You don't have to be great to start, but you have to start to be great.

- When you want to make your life feel better, make your thoughts more positive.

- Today's accomplishments were yesterday's impossibilities.

- Love yourself. It is important to stay positive because beauty comes from the inside out.

- Don't let yesterday take up too much of today.

- You only live once, but if you do it right, once is enough.

- Choosing to be positive and having a grateful attitude is going to determine how you are going to live your life.

- Get busy living or get busy dying.

- Because of your smile, you make life more beautiful.

- Do not take life too seriously. You will never get out of it alive.

- Positivity, confidence, and persistence are key in life, so never give up on yourself.

- Very little is needed to make a happy life; it is all within yourself, in your way of thinking.

- Believe you can and you are halfway there.

- Be happy for this moment. This moment is your life.

- The key to success is to focus on goals, not obstacles.

- Life can only be understood backward; but it must be lived forwards.

- No one can make you feel inferior without your consent.

- Not how long, but how well you have lived is the main thing.

- One day your life will flash before your eyes. Make sure it's worth watching.

- I love those who can smile in trouble.

- It's going to be hard, but hard does not mean impossible.

- Don't stop when you're tired. Stop when you're done.

- Little things make big days.

- Dream bigger. Do bigger.

- Do something today that your future self will thank you for.

- The harder you work for something, the greater you'll feel when you achieve it.

- Wake up with determination and go to bed with satisfaction.

- Success doesn't just find you. You have to go out and get it.

- Dream it. Wish it. Do it.

- Your limitation – It's only your imagination.

- Great minds have purposes, others have wishes.

- Sometimes later becomes never. Do it now.

- The secret of success is constancy to purpose.

- Push yourself, because no one else is going to do it for you.

- Life is like riding a bicycle. To keep your balance, you must keep moving.

- If everything is perfect, you would never learn and you would never grow.

- Difficult roads often lead to beautiful destinations.

- Small steps in the right direction can turn out to be the biggest step of your life.

- Sometimes you will never know the value of a moment until it becomes a memory.

- You can't go back and change the beginning, but you can start where you are and change the ending.

- A diamond is a chunk of coal that did well under pressure.

- Nothing can dim the light that shines from within.

- I am thankful for all of those who said no to me. It's because of them I am doing it myself.

- Talk to yourself, in the same way, would to someone you love.

- Even the greatest were beginners. Don't be afraid to take that first step.

- Your positive action combined with positive thinking results in success.

- I am in charge of how I feel and today I am feeling happiness.

- Life is about making an impact, not making an income.

- With confidence, you have won before you have started.

- The pain you feel today is the strength you feel tomorrow.
- Whatever the mind of man can conceive and believe, it can achieve.
- Confidence is not 'They will like' confidence is 'I'll be fine if they don't'
- The worst enemy to creativity is self-doubt.
- I attribute my success to this: I never gave or took any excuse.
- The meaning of life is to give life meaning.
- May your choices reflect your hopes, not your fears.
- I will remember and recover, not forgive and forget.
- Let the beauty of what you love to be what you do.
- If the world was blind how many people would you impress?
- Time is always right to do what is right.
- It hurt because it mattered.
- Change the game, don't let the game change you.
- Life becomes easier when you learn to accept the apology you never got.

- White is not always light and black is not always dark.

- The good life is inspired by love and guided by knowledge.

- A happy soul is the best shield for a cruel world.

- Think of all the beauty still left around you and be happy.

- Life is a process. We are a process. The universe is a process.

- A mistake that makes you HUMBLE is much better than an ACHIEVEMENT that makes you ARROGANT.

- Pain is a gift. Instead of avoiding it, learn to embrace it. Without pain, there is no growth.

- Sometimes the best thing you can do is keep your mouth shut and your eyes open. The truth always comes out in the end. Be strong enough to focus on what truly matters.

- 8 things to give up: 1) Doubting yourself. 2) Negative thinking. 3) Fear of failure. 4) Criticizing others. 5) Negative self-talk. 6) Procrastination. 7) Fear of success. 8) People pleasing.

- If you have a family that loves you, a few good friends, food on your table and a roof over your head. You are richer than you think.

- There are two types of pain in this world: Pain that hurts you, and pain that changes you.

- No matter how badly someone treats you, never drop down to their level. Remain calm, stay strong, and walk away.

- When I was a child, I was afraid of ghosts. As I grew up, I realized people are scarier.

Chapter 7: Peace and Worry

- Peace begins when the expectations end.

- Peace comes from within. Do not seek it without.

- Forgive others, not because they deserve forgiveness, but because you deserve peace.

- Health does not always come from medicine. Most of the time it comes from peace of mind, peace in the heart, peace of the soul. It comes from laughter and love.

- The only way to bring PEACE to the earth is to learn to make our own life PEACEFUL.

- Be selective in your battles. Sometimes peace is better than being right.

- Nothing will bring you greater peace than minding your own business.

- We can never obtain PEACE in the outer world until we make PEACE with ourselves.

- Resolutely train yourself to attain peace.

- There is no greater wealth in this world than peace of mind.

- Anything that costs you your peace is too expensive. Learn to let it go.

- If there is a solution to your problem, then there is no need to worry. If there is no solution to your problem there is no point to worry.

- Everything that has a beginning has an ending. Make your PEACE with that and all will be well.

- When you find PEACE within yourself, you become the kind of person who can live at PEACE with others.

- To find peace, sometimes you have to be willing to lose your connection with the people, places, and things that create all the noise in your life.

- At the end of the day, I'm at peace, because my intentions are good and my heart is pure.

- Having PEACE of mind is not a strenuous job, it is an effortless process to keep your mind cool and have a great life ahead.

- Promise yourself to be so strong that nothing can disturb your PEACE of mind.

- Better than a thousand hollow words, is one word that brings peace.

- The less you respond to negative people, the more peaceful your life will become.

- PEACE is not the absence of power; PEACE is the presence of love.

- PEACE is not the absence of conflict it is the ability to handle conflict by PEACEFUL means.

- PEACE in my heart, PEACE in my soul, wherever I'm going I'm already home.

- Inner peace begins the moment you choose not to allow another person or event to control your emotions.

- PEACE begins with love and respect.

- PEACE begins when the expectation ends.

- Those who are free of resentful thoughts surely find PEACE.

- Patience is not the ability to wait, but the ability to keep a good attitude while waiting.

- You can't always have a good day. But you can always face a bad day with a good attitude.

- Prayer is talking to the universe. Meditation is listening to it.

- When you let go, you create space for better things to enter your life.

- When you find no solution to a problem, it's probably not a problem to be solved, but rather a truth to be accepted.

- When you face difficult times, know that challenges are not sent to destroy you. They're sent to promote, increase and strengthen you.

- If you saw the size of the blessing that is coming, you would understand the magnitude of the battle you are fighting.

- Falling down is part of life. Getting back up is living.

- Never let your fear decide your future.

- Slow down and enjoy the journey right now. Take time for the people in your life. They won't always be there.

- Be happy at the moment, that's enough. Each moment is all we need, not more.

- He who does not understands your silence will probably not understand your words.

- Be Kind, for everyone you meet is fighting a battle you know nothing about.

- You will never be happy if you are always worried about what others think about you.

- Go easy on yourself. Whatever you do today, let it be enough.

- Loneliness is dangerous. It's addicting. Once you see how peaceful it is, you don't want to deal with people.

- Peace comes from within, do not see it without.

- Beauty catches the attention but the character catches the heart.

- Do not learn how to react learn how to respond.

- Don't think too much. Just do what makes you happy.

- "Happiness" starts with you. Not with your relationships, not with your job, not with your money, but with you.

- Patience is bitter, but its fruit is sweet.

- Peace does not mean an absence of conflict; differences will always be there. Peace means solving these differences through peaceful means; through dialogue, education, knowledge and humane ways.

- If you want to know someone's mind listen to their words. If you want to know their heart watch their actions.

- Fake people have an image to maintain. Real people just don't care.

- People are not as beautiful as they look, as they walk, or as they talk. They are only as beautiful as they love, as they care and as they share.

- When it hurts, observer. Life is teaching you something.

- You are strong when you know your weaknesses. You are beautiful when you appreciate your flaws. You are wise when you learn from your mistakes.

- In a world full of copies, be original.

- Sometimes I go out and hear people talk about irrelevant things and then I tell myself this why I don't go out.

- If there were a mountain made of gold, made entirely of solid gold, Not double this would suffice for one. Having known this, go peacefully.

- Money is the worst discovery of human life. But it is the most trusted material to test human nature.

- People often confuse ego with self-respect.

- Do everything with a good heart and expect nothing in return and you will never be disappointed.

- Never believe you are above or below anyone. Keep a humble spirit.

- You have to fight through some bad days to earn the best days of your life.

- I trust the next chapter because I am the author.

- Speak only when you feel your words are better than your silence.

- In eastern tradition, the mind said to be the cause of our bondage and the cause of our liberation.

- It's in the mind that the entire field of spirituality plays out. But many aspects of the mind is not considered a necessary part of its functions, in particular, worrying is taught to be one of the lowest things we can do.

- To stop worrying is tough, but it's not impossible. If we adopt a few notions of worrying from the Buddhists, an astounding change can take place.

- 1) Understand the mind: It's common knowledge that the best analogy to the human mind is a monkey. They love jumping from one tree to another, similar to how the mind jumps from one thought to another.

- 1) When something attention-grabbing comes up, the mind naturally wants to think about; the only problem is that it easily slides into worrying. This requires awareness in order to stop it.

- 2) Walk Away: The more you worry, the more you agitated. We get wrapped up in something that may not even necessarily exist. The important thing is to take a step back and get out of that energetic 'space' by letting go of that thought pattern, or even walk for a bit. This will help you see it from a different angle, and with a more objective lens.

* 3) Know it Doesn't help: In of itself, worrying doesn't help anything. Think of all the times you worried about things in the past. Notice how you are in the present moment with your current worry, and ask yourself if it will be any different.

* 4) Stop searching for a solution: We worry because we feel out of control in certain situations. We are searching for a way to feel in control again. The uncertainty can be hard for the ego to accept. Instead of fighting that uncertainty, learn to embrace it. You cannot control everything and the universe operates on change. It's a hard truth, but that defines our life. Whether we want it to or not.

* 5) Mindfulness: When we practice mindfulness, we actually allow things to fall into places. We swim in the present moment, part of us deep inside is detached from the outcome. It gives us a sense of peace and contentment. Things flow easier when we don't push them to happen.

Chapter 8: Anger

- You are the first victim of your own anger.
- Where is ANGER, there is always pain underneath.
- No anger inside means no enemy outside.
- Life is an illusion, a dream, a bubble, a shadow, nothing is permanent, nothing is worthy of anger. Nothing is worthy of dispute.
- An outside enemy exists only if there is anger inside.
- Try to manage your ANGER since people can't manage their stupidity.
- ANGER is nothing more than an outward expression of hurt, fear, and frustration.
- ANGER doesn't solve anything it builds nothing, but it can destroy everything.
- If you are patient in one moment of ANGER, you will escape a hundred days of sorrow.
- ANGER is a sign that something needs to change.
- Patience is not a sign of weakness. It is anger that is the sign of weakness, whereas patience is a sign of strength.

- Forgive people in your life, even those who are not sorry for their actions.

- Holding on to ANGER only hurts you, not them.

- You will not be punished for your ANGER; you will be punished by your ANGER.

- To be ANGER is to revenge of the others on ourselves.

- Make your anger so expensive that no one can afford it and make your happiness so cheap that people can almost get it free.

- Holding on to ANGER is like drinking poison and expecting the other person to die.

- Identifying the true root causes of your ANGER can take a lot of courage.

- Whoever doesn't flare up at someone who's ANGER wins a battle hard to win.

- Explain your ANGER, don't express it, and you will immediately open the door to solutions instead of arguments.

- Don't promise when you are happy. Do not reply when you are ANGER and do not decide when you are sad.

- Holding on to anger is like grasping a hot coal with the intent of throwing it at someone else; you are the one who gets burned.

- The more ANGER you carry in your heart towards the past, the less capable you are of loving in the present.

- Our mind is full of ANGER, jealousy, and other negative feelings. Yet we do not realize that these are incompatible with inner peace and joy.

- Consider how much more you often suffer from your ANGER and grief, than from those very things for which you are angry and grieved.

- Hold your worlds when you are angry because sometimes words spoken in ANGER leave a scar that can never be healed.

- Nobody makes you angry you decide to use ANGER as a response.

- There is no enemy outside our soul. The real enemies live inside us: ANGER, EGO, GREED, and HATE.

- Anger is the feeling that makes your mouth work faster than your mind.

Chapter 9: Karma

- KARMA has no menu. You get served what you deserved.

- Don't waste your time on Revenge. Those who hurt you will eventually face their own KARMA.

- Your worst enemy cannot harm you as much as your own unguarded KARMA.

- "You will not understand the damage you did until some else does the same to you, that's why I'm here" – KARMA.

- You will not be punished for your sin; you will be punished by your sin.

- KARMA said, "You will fall in love with someone who doesn't live you, for not loving someone who did."

- What you send out, that will come back. What you sow, you reap. What you give, you get. What you see in others, exists in you. Do not judge anyone, so you will not be judged. Radiate and give love, and love comes back to you its KARMA.

- How people treat you is their KARMA, how you reach is your KARMA.

- You are free to make any decision you wish. But you are not free from the consequences of that decision.

- One day you will realize the damages being done to you are your own KARMA.

- What goes around comes around. Keep your circle positive. Say good words, think good thoughts, do good deeds.

- When a bird is alive. It ears ants when the bird has died, ants eat it.

- When a tree can be made into million matchsticks but the only matchstick is needed to burn a million trees.

- Circumstances can change at any time. Don't devalue or hurt anyone in this life.

- You may be powerful today but time is more powerful than you.

- Your future your karma, your dharma rests on the thoughts and intentions you from today.

- Just because I didn't say anything doesn't mean I didn't notice. Karma will handle it.

- Just nothing, you will be happy. Forgive everything, you will be happier. Love everything, you will be happiest.

- What you put out will come back to you in unexpected ways. Give only what you don't mind getting back to you.

- The best revenge is always to just happily move on and let karma do the rest.

- Everything happens for a reason. But sometimes the reason is that you are stupid and you make bad decisions.

- Nothing happens for by chance, by fate. You create your own fate by your actions that's KARMA.

Chapter 10: Meditation

- Meditation means dissolving the invisible walls that unawareness has built.

- The goal of meditation isn't to control your thoughts, it's to stop letting them control you.

- Meditate. Live purely. Be quiet. Do your work with mastery. Like the moon, come out from behind the clouds and shine.

- Meditation is the tongue of the soul and the language of our spirit.

- Where there are peace and mediation, there is neither anxiety nor doubt.

- The things that trouble our spirits are within us already. In meditation, we must face them, accept them, and set them aside one by one.

- Buddha was asked, "what have you gained from meditation?" He replied, nothing! Buddha said, let tell you what I lost: Anger, Anxiety, depression, insecurity, fear of old age and death.

- The thing about meditation is: you become more and more you.

- Prayer is when you talk to God; meditation is when you listen to God.

- Meditation is a silent heart, A peaceful mind which can make life more lovable, more livable.

- Meditation is bringing the mind at home.

- Over there are the roots of trees; over there empty dwellings. Practice mediation! Don't be heedless!

- Meditate. do not delay, lest you later regret it.

- Meditation releases control over the thoughts in your mind.

- Meditation brings wisdom; lack of meditation leaves ignorance. Know well what leads you forward and what hold you back, and choose the path that leads to wisdom.

Chapter 11: Life Lesson

- Don't compare your life to others, there's no comparison between the sun and the moon. They shine when it's their time.

- Life doesn't allow us to go back and fix what we have done wrong in the past, but it does allow us to live each day better than our last.

- Never force anything. Just let it be. If it's meant to be, it will be.

- All human unhappiness comes from not facing reality squarely. Exactly as it is.

- Without respect, love is lost. Without caring, love is boring. Without honesty, love is unhappy. Without trust, love is unstable.

- Life is such a great teacher that when you don't learn a lesson, it will repeat it.

- A happy person is happy, not because everything is right in his life. He is happy because his attitude towards everything in his life is right.

- If you truly want to change your life, you first must be willing to change your mind.

- Failure is part of life. If you don't fail, you don't learn. If you don't learn you'll never succeed.

- Everybody wants to change the world, but nobody wants to start with themselves.

- If you stand for a reason, be prepared to stand alone like a tree, and if you fall on the ground, fall like a seed that grows back to fight again.

- Be kind, be honest, be loving, be true and all of these things will come back to you.

- If you cannot find peace within yourself, you will never find it anywhere else.

- The problem with closed-minded people is that their mouth is always open

- Never stop trying. Never stop believing. Never give up. Your day will come.

- Never lose faith in yourself; you can do anything in the universe.

- If you focus on the hurt, you will continue to suffer. If you focus on the lesson, you will continue to grow.

- If there is no struggle, there is no progress.

- People talk behind your back for 3 reasons: 1) When they can't reach your level. 2) When they don't have what you have. 3) When they try to copy your lifestyle but can't.

- You will never be brave if you don't get hurt.

- You will never learn if you don't make mistakes.

- You will never be successful if you don't encounter failure.

- We cannot change anything unless we accept it.

- When you talk, you are only repeating what you already know. But if you listen, you may learn something new.

- No great things can be achieved from the comfort zone.

- Anything which is troubling you, anything which is irritating you, that is your teacher.

- Miserable people focus on the things they hate about their life. Happy people focus on the things they love about their life.

- Never judge someone by the opinion of others.

- They will never understand until it happens to them.

- Life is a circle of happiness, sadness, hard times, and good times. If you are going through a hard time, have faith that good times are coming.

- Raise your words, not voice. It is rain that grows flowers, not thunder.

- Stop telling people more than they need to know.

- A wise man never knows all, only fools know everything.

- Feelings are just visitors. Let them come and go.

- How people treat other people is the direct reflection of how they feel about themselves.

- I am not what you think I am. You are what you think I am.

- Your own expectations hurt you more than anything else.

- Hope is the one thing that is stronger than fear.

- Don't wait for someone to bring you flowers. Plant your own garden and decorate your own soul.

- People change for two reasons: either their minds have been opened or their hearts have been broken.

- Freedom comes when you stop caring about what others think of you.

- If you believe you are right but still people criticize you, hurt you, shout at you, don't bother. Just remember, in every game the only audience makes a noise, not players. Be a player believe in yourself and do the best.

- There are three solutions to every problem: Accept it. Change It. Leave it. If you can't accept it, change it. If you can't change it, Leave it.

- It's never too late for a new beginning in your life

- Do not correct a fool, or he will hate you; correct a wise man, and he will appreciate you.

- Like me or hate me both are in my favor. If you like me, I'm in your heart. If you hate me, I'm in your mind.

- Conquer the angry one by not getting angry; conquer the wicked by goodness; conquer the stingy by generosity, and the liar by speaking the truth.

- If you can't change a situation, change your perception of it. Remember, most of your stress comes from the way you respond, not the way life is.

- The first to apologize is the bravest. The first to forgive is the strongest. And the first to forget is the happiest.

- Don't go with the flow. Be the flow.

- My goal is not to be better than anyone else, but to be better than I used to be.

- Don't hate jealous people. They are jealous because they think you are better than them.

* The problem is not the problem. The problem is the incredible amount of over-thinking you're doing with the problem. Let is go and be free.

Chapter 12: Positive Mind

- Positivity is a choice.

- Whoever is trying to bring you down, is already below you.

- One day, you will be at the place you always wanted to be. Don't stop believing.

- Positive people also have negative thoughts. They just don't allow those thoughts to control them.

- You can run from the world, but you can't run from yourself.

- Life is short. Spend it with people who make you laugh and feel loved.

- Tomorrow never comes, it is always today.

- It's your road and yours alone. Others may walk it with you, but no one will walk it for you. No matter what path you are walking.

- Once a year, go someplace you've never been before.

- Don't ask why people hurting you. Ask yourself why you are allowing.

- Strong people don't put others down. They lift them up.

- If your heart has peace, nothing can disturb you.

- Everything seems impossible until it has done.

- If you truly loved yourself, you could never hurt another.

- It is better to travel well than to arrive.

- Focus on the people who inspire you, not the one who annoys you.

- When you wish good for others, good things come back to you. This is the law of nature.

- Don't use your energy to worry. Use your energy to believe.

- The past will be your teacher if you learn from it. You're master if you live in it.

- When you think everything is someone else's fault, you will suffer a lot.

- If people treated you like an option, leave them like a choice.

- Learn from yesterday. live for today. Hope for tomorrow.

- 4 things you can never recover in Life: 1) A word after it's spoken 2) An Opportunity after it's missed. 3) Time after it's gone. 4) Trust after it's lost.

- What comes easy, won't last long. And what lasts longer, won't come easy.

- Education is the most powerful tool to change the world.

- Count your blessings, not your problems.

- The true hero is one who conquers his own anger and hatred.

- Help when you can. Be there you can. Encourage when you can. A truly happy life comes from giving more than you take.

- You are the problem. And only you are the solution.

- What people think about you is not important. What you think about yourself means everything.

- Mistakes are painful when they happen. But years later a collection of mistakes called experience which leads us to success.

- Never get too attached to someone, because attachment leads to expectation and expectations lead to disappointment.

- We must train the mind to always see the good.

- "Sorry" works when a mistake is made, but not when trust is broken. So, in life, make mistakes but never break trust.

Because forgiving is easy, but forgetting and trusting again is something impossible.

* Do everything with a good heart and expect nothing in return, and you will never be disappointed.

* Money is numbers and numbers never end. If it takes money to be happy, your search for happiness will never end.

* Always remember that your present situation is not your final destination. The best is yet to come.

* I don't care what people think or say about me, I know who I am, and I don't have to prove anything to anyone.

* Life always offers you a second chance: TOMORROW!

* No poison can kill a positive thinker, and no medicine can save a negative thinker.

* The most expensive thing in the world is TRUST. It can take years to earn and a matter of seconds to lose.

* Pain makes you stronger, tears make you braver, and heartbreaks make you wiser, so than the past for a better future.

Chapter 13: Loneliness

- It's better to be unhappy alone than unhappy with someone.

- You can't be strong all the time. Sometimes you just need to be alone and let your tears out.

- The time you feel lonely is the time you most need to be by yourself.

- People think being alone makes you lonely, but that's not true. Being surrounded by the wrong people is the loneliest thing in the world.

- Loneliness is better than bad company.

- Standing alone doesn't mean I am alone. It means I am strong enough to handle things all by myself.

- I prefer loneliness over the fake company.

- Learn to enjoy being alone. Because no one will stay forever.

- It is easy to stand in the crowd but it takes courage to stand alone.

- Stand up for what you believe in, even if it means standing alone.

- We came into the world alone; we will also leave the world alone. So, it's better to be alone now.

- Sometimes you need to be alone. Not be lonely, but to enjoy your free time being yourself.

- You are never alone. You are eternally connected with everyone.

- Sometimes you need to break from everyone and spend time alone, to experience, appreciate and love yourself.

- If you make a friend with yourself you will never be alone.

- Pray that your loneliness may spur you into finding something to live for, great enough to die for.

- Letting go means, to come to the realization that some people are a part of your history, but not a part of your destiny.

- Everything happens for a reason. Don't question it, trust it.

Chapter 14: Happiness

- There is no path of happiness, happiness is the path.

- Stop looking for happiness in the same place you lost it.

- You will never happy if you continue to hold on to the things that make you sad.

- The key to happiness: focus on your own journey.

- Seven steps to Happiness: 1) Think less and feel more. 2) Frown less, smile more. 3) Talk less and listen more. 4) Judge less, accept more. 5) Watch less, do more. 6) Complain less, appreciate more. 7) Fear less, love more.

- I have stopped explaining myself when I realized people only understand from their level of perception.

- Happiness is found when you stop comparing yourself to other people.

- There are two ways to be happy; Change your situation or change your mindset towards it.

- Sometimes you just have to let go and see what happens.

- The less you care, the happier you will be.

- People get MAD at you when they can't use you.

- Common sense is a flower that doesn't grow in everyone's garden.

- 10 things money can't buy: Manners, morals, respect, character, common sense, trust, patience, class, integrity, Love.

- Six rules to be happy life: 1) Never hate. 2) Don't worry. 3) Live simple. 4) Expect a little. 5) Give a lot. 6) And always smile.

- When you try to control everything, you enjoy nothing. Sometimes, you just need to relax, breathe, let go and live in the moment.

- To be happy you must: 1) Let go of what's gone. 2) Be grateful for what remains. 3) Look forward to what's coming next.

- With understanding and loving-kindness, we will look within ourselves, we will find happiness, wisdom, and serenity.

- If you've never tasted a bad apple, you won't appreciate a good apple. You need to experience life to understand life.

- If there are no ups and downs in life it means you are dead.

- Life is short. Time is fast. No replay, no rewind. Enjoy every moment as it comes.

- Happiness starts with you. Not with your relationships, not with your jobs, not with your money, but with you.

- Don't close the book when bad things happen in your life. Turn the page and start a new chapter.

- Be strong but no rude.

- Be kind but not weak.

- Be bold but not a bully.

- Be humble but not timid.

- Be proud but not arrogant.

- The secret of change is to focus all of your energy, not on fighting the old, but on building the new.

- It's your life! Don't let anyone make you feel guilty for living it your way.

- You don't have a soul. You are a soul. You have a body.

- Before you speak "Think" Is it True? Is it Helpful? Is it Inspiring? Is it Necessary? Is it Kind?

- You have a past, but don't live there anymore.

- Before going to sleep every night, forgive everyone, and sleep with a clean heart.

- The only thing you can really control is how you react to things out of your control.

- Win in your mind and you will win in your reality.

- Forgive those who insult you, attack you, belittle you or take you for granted. But more than this, forgive yourself for allowing them to hurt you.

- Trust is like a paper, once it's crumpled it can't be perfect again.

- The trouble is, you think you have time.

- Be deaf to negative thoughts. If your aim is to reach your goal.

- No amount of guilt can solve the past and no amount of anxiety can change the future.

- Confuse them with your silence, Amaze them with your actions.

- Stress is not what happens to us. It's our response to what happens and response is something we can choose.

- Look within. The secret is within you.

- Don't carry your mistakes around with you. Instead, place them under your feet and use them as stepping stones to rise above them.

- Give people time. Give people space. Don't beg anyone to stay. Let them roam. What's meant for you will always be yours.

- Keep your thoughts positive because your thoughts become your words.

- Keep your word positive because your words become your behavior.

- Keep your behavior positive because your behavior becomes your habits.

- Keep your habits positive because your habits become your values.

- Keep your values positive because your values become your destiny.

- Learn from everyone. Follow no one.

- Sometimes it feels better not to talk at all, about anything to anyone.

- If you can learn self-control you can master anything.

- Stress is the gap between expectation and reality. More the gap, the more the stress. So, expect nothing and accept everything.

- Life is beautiful. One day, one hour, and one minute will not come again in your entire life. Avoid fight, angriness and speak lovely to every person.

- Prove yourself to yourself, not others.

- Start where you are. Use what you have. Do what you can.

- The happiest people don't have the best of everything, they just make the best of everything they have.

- Train your mind to be calm in every situation.

- Set an Example: Treat everyone with kindness and respect even those who are rude to you. Not because they are nice, but because you are.

- The greatest gift you can give someone is your time. Because when you give your time, you are giving a portion of your life that you will never get back.

- Maturity is learning to walk away from people, and situations that threaten your peace of mind, self-respect, values morals and self-worth.

- Be an example. Show kindness to unkind people. Forgive people who don't deserve it. Love unconditionally. Your actions always reflect who you are.

- Before getting upset always ask yourself: Will this even matter in the next six months, in a year, or in five years? If the answer is No. JUST LET IT GO.

- The only keeper of your happiness is you. Stop giving people the power to control your simile, your worth and your attitude.

- We can't help everyone, but everyone can help someone.

- Smiling is the best way to face every problem, to crush every fear, to hind every pain.

- Sometimes people with the worst pasts end up creating best the future.

- Pain is certain, suffering is optional.

- To conquer oneself is a greater task than conquering others.

- Every human being is the author of his own health or disease.

- Work out your own salvation, do not depend on others.

- In the end, these things matter most: How well did you love? How fully did you live? How deeply did you let go?

- To keep the body in good health is a duty otherwise we shall not be able to keep our mind strong and clear.

- A generous heart, kind speech, a life of service and compassion are the things which renew humanity.

- Happy is entirely up to you and always has been.

- Yesterday is History, Tomorrow is a mystery, Today is a gift (Present).

- There is only one person who could ever make you happy, and that person is you.

- The only medicine for suffering, crime, and all the other woes of mankind is wisdom (awareness).

- All the joy the world contains has come through wishing happiness for others.

- All the misery the world contains has come from wishing pleasure for oneself.

- Constant kindness can accomplish much. As the sun makes ice melt, kindness causes misunderstanding, mistrust, and hostility to evaporate.

- Develop the quiet, even state of mind when praised by some and condemned by others.

- Free the mind from hate and pride, and gently go your way in peace.

- Even if everyone else is not doing good, I alone will. Even if everyone else is doing wrong, I alone will not.

- We already have perfect compassion, perfect wisdom, perfect joy, we only need to settle our minds, so that can arise from deep within us.

- Focus not on the rudeness of others, not on what they've done, or left undone, but on what you have and have not done yourself.

- When we free ourselves of desires, we will know serenity and freedom. Avoid all evil, embrace all goodness, purifies one's own mind.

- Nobody can make you happy until you're happy with yourself first.

- Judge nothing, you will be happy. Forgive everything, you will be happier. Love everything, you will be happiest.

- Happiness is not the absence of problems but the ability to deal with them.

- Happiness does not depend on what you have or what you are. It solely relies on what you think.

- Nothing can bring happiness but yourself.

Chapter 15: Mind and Mindfulness

- The mind is a beautiful servant, but a dangerous master.

- Train your mind to see good in every situation.

- Your mind will always believe everything you tell it. Feed it with faith. Feed it with the truth. Feed it with love.

- Empty minds make the most noise.

- What consumes your mind controls your life.

- Your mind is a magnet. You think of problems, you attract problems. But if you think of blessings, you attract blessings.

- The Mind precedes all mental states. The mind is the chief; they are all mind-wrought. If with an impure mind a person speaks or acts suffering follows him like the wheel that follows the foot of the ox.

- The Mind precedes all mental states. The mind is the chief; they are all mind-wrought. If with a pure mind a person speaks or acts happiness follows him like he's never departing shadow.

- "He abused me, he struck me, he overpowered me, he robbed me." Those who harbor such thoughts do not still their hatred.

- If a man's mind becomes pure, his surroundings will also become pure.

- Hatred is never appeased by hatred in this world. Buying non-hatred alone is hatred appeased this is a law of eternal.

- There are those who do not realize that one day will all die. But those who do realize this set to their quarrels.

- Just as a storm throws down a weak tree, so does Mara overpower the man who lives for the pursuit of pleasures, who is uncontrolled in his senses, immoderate in eating, indolent, and dissipated.

- Just as a storm cannot prevail against a rocky mountain, so Mara can never overpower the man who lives meditating on the impurities, who is controlled in his senses, moderate in eating and filled with faith and earnest effort.

- Whoever being depraved, devoid of self-control and truthfulness, should don the monk's yellow robe, he surely is not worthy of the robe. But whoever is purged of depravity, well-established in virtues and filled with self-control and truthfulness, he indeed is worthy of the yellow robe.

- Those who mistake the unessential to be essential and the essential to be unessential, dwelling in wrong thoughts, never arrive at the essential.

- Those who know the essential be the essential and the unessential to be unessential, dwelling in the right thoughts, do arrive at the essential.

- Just as rain breaks through an ill-thatched house, so passion penetrates an undeveloped mind.

- Just as rain does not break through a well-thatched house, so passion never penetrates a well-developed mind.

- The evil-doer grieves here and hereafter; he grieves in both the worlds. He laments and is afflicted recollecting his own impure deeds.

- The doer of good rejoices here and hereafter; he rejoices in both the world. He rejoices and exults, recollecting his own pure deeds.

- The evil-doer suffers here and hereafter; The thought, "Evil have I done" torments him, and he suffers even more when gone to realms of woe.

- The doer of good delights here and hereafter; he delights in both the worlds. The thought, "Good have I done", delights him, and he delights even more when to realms of bliss.

- Much though he recites the sacred texts, but act not accordingly, that heedless man is like a cowherd, who only counts the cows of others. He does not partake in the blessing of a holy life.

* Little though he recites the sacred texts, but puts the teachings into practice, forsaking lust, hatred, and delusion, with true wisdom and emancipated mind, clinging to nothing of this or another world he indeed partakes of the blessings of a holy life.

* Heedfulness is the path to the deathless. Heedlessness is the path to death.

* The heedful die not. The heedless are as if dead already.

* Clearly understanding this excellence of heedfulness, the wise exult therein and enjoy the resort of the noble ones.

* The secret of health for both mind and body is not to mourn for the past, worry about the future or anticipate troubles but to live in the present moment wisely and earnestly.

* Heart of a Buddha, to be honorable in thoughts, sincere in words, Kind in deeds, is to have a heart of a Buddha.

* The wise ones, ever meditative and steadfastly preserving, alone experience Nibbana, the incomparable freedom from bondage.

- Ever grows the glory of him who energetic, mindful and pure in conduct, discerning and self-controlled, righteous and heedful.

- By effort and heedfulness, discipline and self-mastery let the wise one makes for himself an island which no flood can overwhelm.

- The foolish and ignorant indulge in heedlessness, but the wise one keeps his heedfulness as his best treasure.

- Do not give way to heedlessness. Do not indulge in sensual pleasures. Only the heedful and meditative attain great happiness.

- Just as one upon the summit of a mountain beholds the groundings, even so, when the wise man casts away heedlessness by heedfulness and ascends the high tower of wisdom, this sorrowless sage beholds the sorrowing and foolish multitude.

- Heedful among the heedless, wide-awake among the sleepy, the wise man advances like a swift horse leaving behind a weak jade.

- By heedfulness did Indra become the overlord of gods. Heedfulness is ever praised, and heedlessness ever despised.

- The monk who delights in heedfulness and looks with fear at heedlessness advances like fire, burning all fetters, small and large.

- The monk who delights in heedfulness and looks with fear at heedlessness will not fall. He is close to Nibbana.

- Just as a fletcher straightens an arrow shaft, even so, the discerning man straightens his mind so fickle and unsteady, so difficult to guard.

- As a fish when pulled out of water and cast on land throbs and quivers, even so, is this mind agitated. Hence should one abandon the realm of Mara.

- Wonderful, indeed, it is to subdue the mind, so difficult to subdue, ever swift, and seizing whatever it desires. A tamed mind brings happiness.

- Let the discerning man guard the mind, so difficult to detect and extremely subdue, seizing whatever it desires. A guarded mind brings happiness.

- Dwelling in the cave of (of the heart), the mind, without form, wanders far and alone. Those who subdue this mind are liberated from the bonds of Mara.

- Wisdom never becomes perfect in one whose mind is not steadfast, who knows not the good teaching and whose faith wavers.

- There is no fear for an awakened one, whose mind is not sodden (by lust) nor afflicted (by hate), and who has gone beyond both merit and demerit.

- Realizing that this body is as fragile as a clay pot, and fortifying this mind like a well-fortified city, fight out Mara (evil) with the sword of wisdom.

- Then, guarding the conquest, remain unattached.

- Ere long, alas! This body will lie upon the earth, unheeded and lifeless, like a useless log.

- Whatever harm an enemy may do to an enemy or a hater to a hater, an ill-directed mind inflicts on oneself a greater harm.

- Neither mother, father, nor any other relative can do one greater good than one's own well-directed mind.

- Who shall overcome this earth, this realm of Yama and this sphere of man and gods? Who shall bring to perfection the well-taught path of wisdom as an expert garland-maker would his floral design?

- A striver-on-the path shall overcome this earth, this realm of Yama and this sphere of man and gods? the striver-on-the path shall bring to perfection. The well-taught path of wisdom as an expert garland-maker would his floral design.

- Realizing that this body is like forth, penetrating its mirage-like nature, and plucking out Mara's flower-tipped arrows of sensuality go beyond sight of the king of death!

- As mighty flood sweeps away the sleeping village, so death sweeps away the person of distracted mind who only plucks the flowers (of pleasure).

- The destroyer brings under his sway the person of distracted mind who, insatiate in sense desires, only plucks the flower (of pleasure).

- As a bee gathers honey from the flower without injuring its color or fragrance, even so, the sage goes on his alms-round in the village.

- Let none find fault with others; let none see the omissions and commissions of others. But let one see one's own acts done and undone.

- Like a beautiful flower full of color but without fragrance, even so, fruitless are the fair words of one who does not practice them.

- Like a beautiful flower full of color and also fragrant, even so, fruitful are the fair words of one who practices them.

- As from a great heap of flowers, many garlands can be made, even so, should many good deeds be done by one born a mortal.

- Not the sweet smell of flowers, not even the fragrance of sandal, tagara, or jasmine blows against the wind. But the fragrance of the virtuous blows against the wind.

- Truly the virtuous man pervades all directions with the fragrance of his virtue.

- Of all the fragrances of sandal, tagara, blue lotus, and jasmine the fragrance of virtue is the sweetest.

- Faint is the fragrance of tagara and sandal, but excellent is the fragrance of the virtuous, wafting even amongst the gods.

- A man never finds the path of the truly virtuous, who abide in heedfulness and are freed by perfect knowledge.

- Upon a heap of rubbish in the road-side ditch blooms a lotus, fragrant and pleasing. even so on the rubbish of blinded mortals, the disciple of the supremely enlightened One shines resplendent in wisdom.

- Long is the night to the sleepless, long is the league to the weary, long is worldly existence to fools who know not the sublime truth.

- Should a seeker find a companion who is better or equal, let him resolutely pursue a solitary course; there is no fellowship with the fool.

- ❃ The fool worries, thinking, "I have sons, I have wealth." Indeed, when he himself not his own, whence are sons, whence is wealth?

- ❃ A fool who knows his foolishness is wise at least to that extent, but a fool who thinks himself wise is a fool indeed.

- ❃ Though all his life a fool associates with a wise man, he no more comprehends the Truth than a spoon tastes the flavor of the soup.

- ❃ Though only for a moment a discerning person associates with a wise man, quickly he comprehends the truth.

- ❃ Fools of little wit are enemies unto themselves as they move about doing evil deeds, the fruits of which are bitter.

- ❃ Ill done is that action of doing which one repents later, and the fruit of which one, weeping, reaps with tears.

- ❃ Well done is that action of doing which one repents later, and the fruits of which one reaps with delight and happiness.

- ❃ So long as an evil deed has not ripened, the fool thinks it as sweet as honey. But when the evil deed ripens, the fool comes to grief.

- ❃ Month after month a fool may eat his food with the tip of a blade of grass, but he still is not worth the sixteenth part of those who have comprehended the truth.

- Truly, an evil deed committed does not immediately bear fruit like milk that does not turn sour all at once. But smoldering, it follows the fool like fire covered by ashes.

- To his own ruin, the fool gains knowledge, for it cleaves his head and destroys his innate goodness.

- The fool seeks undeserved reputation, precedence among monks, authority over monasteries, and honors among householders.

- "Let both layman and monks think that it was done by me. In every work great, and small, let them follow me" – such is the ambition of the fool thus his desire and pride increase.

- One is the quest for worldly gain, and quite another is the path to Nibbana. Clearly understanding this, let not the monk, the disciple of the Buddha.

- Be carried away by worldly acclaim but develop detachment indeed.

- Should one find a man who points out faults and who reproves, let him follow such a wise and sagacious person as one would guide to hidden treasure. It is always better, and never worse, to cultivate such an association. Let him admonish, instruct and shield one from wrong; he, indeed, is dear to the good and detestable to the evil.

- Do not associate with evil companions; do not seek the fellowship of the vile. Associate with good friends; seek the fellowship of a noble man.

- He who thinks deep the Dhamma lives happily with a tranquil mind. The wise man ever delights in the Dhamma made known by the Noble One (the Buddha).

- Irrigators regulate the rivers; fletchers straighten the arrow shaft; carpenters shape the wood; the wise control themselves.

- Just as a solid rock is not shaken by the storm even so the wise are not affected by praise or blame.

- On hearing the teachings, the wise become, perfectly purified like a lake deep, clear and still.

- The good renounce (attachment for) everything. The virtuous do not prattle with a yearning for pleasures. The wise show no elation or depression when touched by happiness or sorrow.

- He is indeed virtuous, wise, and righteous who neither for his own sake nor for the sake of another (does any wrong) who does not crave for sons, wealth, or kingdom, and does not desire success by unjust means.

- Few among men are those who cross to the farther shore. The rest, the bulk of men, only run up and down the hither bank. But those who act accordingly to the perfectly taught Dhamma will cross the realm of death, so difficult to cross.

- Abandoning the dark way, let the wise man had gone from home to homelessness, let him yearn for that delight in detachment, so difficult to enjoy.

- Giving up sensual pleasures, with no attachment, let the wise man cleanse himself of defilements of the mind.

- Those whose minds have reached full excellence in the factors of enlightenment, who, having renounced acquisitiveness, rejoice in not clinging to things

- Rid of cankers, glowing with wisdom, they have attained Nibbana in this very life.

Made in the USA
Coppell, TX
19 February 2020